Guidebooks for Counsell<

GW00362878

Counsellors in the course of their practice ar
particular difficulties, such as experience o
or eating difficulties. These issues may not b
and it may not be appropriate to refer the cli
fields, if such exists locally. There may be literature available but little guidance
for the counsellor seeking it.

The Publications Sub-Committee of the British Association for Counselling are
publishing a series of booklets to help counsellors in this situation. Written
by specialist counsellors or therapists, they draw attention to issues which are
likely to arise for the client and for the counsellor and which may be missed by
the novice. They also provide a guide to the relevant literature. Being brief,
readable and to the point it is hoped that counsellors will be able to consult them
even when time and money are short. In this way it is hoped that these booklets
will contribute to the raising of standards of counselling in general.

The Sub-Committee would like to thank not only those members who worked
to produce these booklets, but also Isobel Palmer and Sally Cook, and the
consultant editors, myself, Gladeana McMahon and Stephen Palmer, whose
contribution was vital.

Julia Segal
Chair, Publications Sub-Committee of the
British Association for Counselling from 1987 to 1993.

Mike Ward

Mike Ward is Purchasing Manager (Alcohol and Drug Services) with Surrey
Social Services and was formerly Director of Surrey Alcohol and Drug
Advisory Service. He is chair of the Alcohol Concern Education and Training
Committee and has been involved in working on both a national qualification
for the alcohol field and a national alcohol training strategy. He is author of
a number of books and articles on topics such as Alcohol Problems in Old Age.
He has advised the Government of Gibraltar on tackling alcohol and drug
problems. He is author of *Taking Drugs or Taking Part* TACADE's book on
drug misuse in sport.

Working with

Problem Drinkers

Mike Ward

British Association for Counselling
1 Regent Place • Rugby • Warwickshire CV21 2PJ
Office 01788 550899 • Information Line 01788 578328 • Fax 01788 562189

© **BAC 1995**   **ISBN 0 946181 48 9**

Published by	British Association for Counselling, 1 Regent Place, Rugby, Warwickshire CV21 2PJ
First printed 1995	
Produced by	BAC, company limited by guarantee 2175320 registered in England & Wales, and registered charity 298361
Printed by	Quorn Litho, Queens Road, Loughborough, Leicestershire LE11 1HH

Other titles in the series

Counselling Adults who were Abused as Children by Peter Dale
Counselling People in Eating Distress by Carole Waskett
Counselling People with Infertility Problems by Sheila Naish

British Association for Counselling

- Codes of Ethics & Practice for Counsellors, for Counselling Skills, for Trainers in Counselling & Counselling Skills and for the Supervision of Counsellors
- Counselling publications mail order service
- Quarterly journal with in-depth articles, news and views of members
- Individual accreditation, supervisor recognition and counsellor training course recognition schemes
    Join BAC now — the Voice of Counselling
    Details of the above and much more besides:
    BAC, 1 Regent Place, Rugby CV21 2PJ. Tel: 01788 550899

Contents

(continued overleaf...)

Foreword

Counsellors are being faced with an increasing number of clients experiencing alcohol-related problems. Whether counselling within an agency setting or in private practice, it is impossible to avoid coming across the negative effects of alcohol on the lives of individuals. Those individuals may be the problem drinkers themselves or their family, friends and work colleagues.

The alcohol field itself has many different approaches to understanding and dealing with the effects of alcohol and there is more than one school of thought on the subject. Mike Ward has written an easy to read, no nonsense, down to earth booklet which provides useful information to help counsellors deal more effectively with clients experiencing problems associated with their alcohol consumption. He has managed to steer a path of common sense through what can, at times, seem like a minefield of conflicting information. In addition, he has managed to treat the subject with sensitivity using examples that the reader can relate to.

Many individuals think of people experiencing alcohol-related problems as being manipulative and hard to work with. Indeed, many an able counsellor has suddenly felt 'de-skilled' when presented with a client whose issues, solely or in part, can be linked to unhelpful alcohol consumption. Mike Ward's booklet provides an anchor for those with little or no experience of dealing with this area of growing need.

Counsellors may also be called upon to help the friends, family and work colleagues of a problem drinker. This booklet will prove of use in assisting the counsellor help those concerned consider the issues surrounding problem drinking and the options available to the problem drinker.

With alcohol misuse on the increase Mike Ward's booklet is needed more now than ever before.

Gladeana McMahon
Counsellor, Trainer, Supervisor
Former Director of Public Relations for Turning Point and
Co-Director, Problem Solving Psychotherapy Programme,
Centre for Stress Management

Why this book has been written

Jancis Robinson, the television wine pundit, maintains that '. . . none of us drinks alcohol. We drink delicious, liberating, inspiring or socially significant liquids which happen to contain alcohol.'[1]

Whatever we may think of alcohol, in 1991 we spent £23,500 million on it in the United Kingdom[2]. This made it the largest item of expenditure after food and housing. Alcohol is clearly a major factor in the UK economy. The facts speak for themselves:

* Around 650,000 people are employed in the production or sale of alcoholic drinks out of a total UK workforce of 25 million[3]. The real number employed may be even greater. The exact size of the UK alcohol industry is hard to determine. Pubs and hotels will often use large numbers of casual staff. How many supermarket staff are employed because of the selling of alcohol and are airline staff who sell duty-free included?

* The 32 largest brewers and distillers had an annual turnover of around £26 billion and made profits of around £3 billion in 1989. The six largest of these companies made £2.7 billion profit in 1989 on a turnover of £23.75 billion4.

* 2% of the UK's exports consist of whisky sales. This is a phenomenal figure and it is increased when beer and other spirit exports are included[3].

* £156 million was spent on advertising alcohol in 1991[2].

* Taxes and duties on alcohol are a major source of tax revenues for the government. In 1987-88 drink tax revenues netted £7.5 billion for the Exchequer. That figure is 4% of total Government income. The advent of the Single European Market may force the Government to think about lowering rates of taxation which could threaten an increase in consumption[3].

On the other hand, in 1990 the UK population drank 7.6 litres of pure alcohol per capita. This places the UK well down the international consumption league table with countries such as France or Luxembourg consuming almost twice as much as the UK[2].

It is often suggested that the consumption of alcohol in the UK is on the increase but the accuracy of this view depends on the time scale examined. Judging by the standards of the last 300 years, current alcohol consumption is at a relatively modest level. On the other hand, since the Second World War alcohol consumption has increased immensely. However, since the early 1980s national consumption of alcohol has risen only gently and as far as beer and spirits are concerned the rise in consumption has flattened out.

Alcohol's economic significance is matched by its social significance. Alcohol plays a huge role in the life of this country and most other western cultures. Alcohol is everywhere, from the launching of a ship to post-match socialising in a sports club. Even the central rite of the major Christian denominations makes use of alcohol.

Yet on the other hand alcohol is a powerful depressant drug, reviled and eschewed by many of the world's religions. It probably causes more harm to western culture than any other drug. Alcohol kills around 30,000 people each year (Heroin claims the lives of about 300-400 people per year). While cigarettes kill far more people, alcohol has a catalogue of associated harms which make it a more troubling drug, for example:
- 45% of woundings and assults and up to 50% of murders are related to alcohol use
- 66% of suicide attempts and deaths are related to alcohol
- 19% of drownings are related to alcohol[8].

Clearly as Jancis Robinson describes it, alcohol is 'the darling demon drink'.[1]

At least one million people are thought to have serious alcohol problems in the UK. Other statistics put the figure much higher. Some have suggested that as many as one in ten people are experiencing problems from their own drinking or someone else's drinking.

When broken down to a local level this data suggests that at least 6,000 people in an average health district of 250,000 people have a serious alcohol problem. On top of those people the Health Education Authority suggests that around 15-20% of the adult population drink over the safe limits (see below).

It is fair to say that the counsellor who doesn't have any clients with alcohol problems is not looking carefully enough. Alcohol problems affect everyone—male or female, young and old, all ethnic groups. The key question is not 'whether counsellors will meet alcohol problems?' but 'what they will do about it when they come across a problem?'

The aim of this book is threefold:
- to help the counsellor identify the problem drinker by giving basic information about the nature of alcohol and alcohol problems.
- to encourage counsellors to raise the issue of alcohol, even if it is only then to refer the client on to another agency.
- to enable counsellors to undertake alcohol counselling with clients if they feel this is appropriate.

Alcohol is a huge problem with many component parts ranging from government policy to the problems of a single individual. Counselling problem drinkers needs to be put in its social and political context. Helping agencies can have a major impact on alcohol misuse, nonetheless there is a vital role for both generic and specialist counsellors in helping people deal with the problems caused by alcohol.

Basic information about alcohol and its effects

Working with problem drinkers need not be more complicated than any other piece of counselling. The counsellor will, however, need to be familiar with certain basic information about alcohol. This is summarised in the next section. The bibliography provides a number of other sources of information. If the counsellor is still in doubt about some aspect of alcohol counselling, the best advice is to contact one of the network of alcohol advice agencies to be found up and down the country.

How much is it safe to drink?

The Strengths of Drinks

One of the most basic pieces of information required by an alcohol counsellor is a picture of the quantity of alcohol being consumed. Yet it is difficult to judge how much someone is drinking because alcohol comes in many different forms. Is the woman consuming two bottles of wine drinking more or less than the man drinking five pints of beer? Is it safe to drink half a bottle of wine or a couple of sherries?

To overcome this problem, a standard measure has been created: **one unit of alcohol**. This is equivalent to
- a single English pub measure (1/6 gill) of spirits
- half a pint of ordinary strength beer (3.5% alcohol)
- a glass of wine (15cl)
- a small schooner of sherry
- a pub measure (1/3 gill) of vermouth

All these have 8 grammes of pure alcohol and thus equal **one unit.**

These measures are a very rough guide and there are a number of exceptions to these equivalent values:

1. Measures of drink poured at home are likely to be much larger than pub measures so it is worth remembering that:
   - a bottle of spirits has 32 units
   - a bottle of sherry has 12 units
   - a bottle of wine has around 6-7 units, depending on strength.

2.   Beers can also be much stronger than one unit to half a pint. There are some beers, e.g. Carlsberg Special Brew or Tennants Extra, which have as much as 2.5 units per half pint. The label on the can or bottle will help determine the strength. Ordinary strength beer is about 3.5% alcohol, so beers stronger than that will have proportionately more units per half pint.

3.   Red wine generally contains more alcohol than white wine. Thus a bottle of red wine will tend to have more units than a bottle of white.

Knowledge of the strengths of the various drinks is only useful if one has a measure of how much it is safe to drink. The Health Education Authority recommends the following maximum levels:

21 units per week for a man
14 units per week for a woman

NB: Women are recommended to drink less both because they tend to be smaller and lighter than men and also because females metabolise alcohol more slowly than males due to the greater proportion of fats in their bloodstream.

Even these safe limits need to be qualified:
- It is not safe to consume all these drinks at once. They should be spread out over the week with one or two drink-free days each week. This is particularly significant for younger people who may consume very little during the week but drink a great deal at the weekend.
- People in poor health or of low body weight may find these limits too high. Thus many elderly people or those who have serious health problems should be set a lower limit, perhaps 10 units for a man and 7 units for a woman.
- Alcohol may need to be avoided if someone is taking drugs, whether these are prescribed or illegal drugs. A fuller list of drugs which react with alcohol is given below.
- Pregnant women or those planning a family may be best advised to avoid alcohol. There is no doubt that alcohol can damage the foetus. There is, however, no clear indication of how much alcohol it takes to affect it. Thus the safest advice may be to avoid alcohol altogether. That said, it is important not to cause unnecessary anxiety or guilt to women who were not abstaining and then found they were one or two months pregnant.

- Most obviously if someone is driving then it may be better to avoid alcohol altogether. This limitation should also apply to anyone using other dangerous or heavy machinery. In particular drinking at lunchtime and then returning to work on a piece of industrial or commercial equipment is a dangerous practice.

Drinking and driving

The law allows the driver to drink a certain amount and still drive. In medical/legal terms this limit is:

a blood alcohol level of 80mg/ml

or

a breath alcohol level of 35mcg/ml

It is helpful but not easy to translate this into units of alcohol. On average these limits equate to:

5 units of alcohol for a man

3 units of alcohol for a woman.

These values are subject to some variation, e.g.
- a large woman could drink more and a small man less, before they were over the legal limit
- on average one unit of alcohol is broken down by the body in about an hour. Some people, however, break alcohol down much more swiftly, others much more slowly. This will have an obvious impact on the various blood alcohol levels.

The legal limit, unfortunately, says nothing about a person's ability to drive. Many people would be completely incapable of driving after drinking less than five units but would still be within the legal limit.

The safest message must be not to drink before driving.

The protective effect of alcohol

The advice on the safe drinking levels are not universally agreed. There is some recent evidence that consumption of alcohol over the safe limits can reduce the risk of heart attacks. This information is clearly controversial and it is hard to know whether safe limits advice should be altered as a consequence.

The view of this booklet, as we shall see in the next section, is that the harmful effects of alcohol are not limited to physical/medical consequences. There are many social consequences which also demand adherence to safe limits. For this reason this booklet will continue to advise the 21/14 unit limits.

Identifying the Problem Drinker

The physical effects of alcohol

Identifying the person with the drink problem is the essential first step in the helping process. As a consequence counsellors could reasonably expect to be given a list of signs and symptoms to aid identification.

This is not easy as almost anything could be a sign of a problem. Any of the following could be signs of drinking:

- a broken leg
- a cheerful mood
- a depressed mood
- isolation
- an active social life

Below we look at factors that make people vulnerable to alcohol and its effects on them. This list could never be exhaustive even if it filled the entire book. Yet the danger of only offering a shorter list is that counsellors may fail to notice less obvious signs of a problem. Instead of slavishly following these lists, it is suggested counsellors draw upon their own existing experiences of working with people. Always bear in mind the possibility of a drinking problem when assessing people. In this way, counsellors will quickly identify people with alcohol problems.

In order to impose some structure on the mass of signs and symptoms presented by problem drinkers this booklet will use a model used widely in the alcohol field[8]. This model clusters the social, physical and psychological effects into three groups:

- problems related to intoxication
- problems related to regular heavy use
- problems related to dependency.

Problems of intoxication

This is probably the least acknowledged and most widespread group of alcohol related problems. There is a high level of awareness of problems associated with 'football hooligans', 'lager louts' and other such instances of a high level of intoxication.

It is important to realise that quite a low level of intoxication can give rise to problems such as drinking and driving, minor domestic accidents, disagreements or hangovers. Everyone is exposed to these problems. One does not have to be a drinker. Being jostled by a drunken lager lout is as much an alcohol related problem as that same lager lout's broken nose obtained in a drunken fight.

The most obvious effects of intoxication are as follows:

family arguments	*criminal damage*
domestic violence	*theft*
child neglect/abuse	*burglary*
domestic accidents	*assault*
absenteeism from work	*homicide*
accidents at work	*drinking and driving*
inefficient work	*taking cars and driving away*
public drunkenness	*road traffic accidents*
public aggression	*sexually deviant acts*
football hooliganism	*unwanted pregnancy*

Although intoxication is primarily associated with acute social problems it may also be associated with a number of physical and psychological problems:

hepatitis	*strokes*
gastritis	*acute alcohol poisoning*
pancreatitis	*failure to take prescribed medication*
gout	*impotence*
cardiac arrythmia	*accidents*
foetal damage	*trauma*
insomnia	*amnesia*
depression	*attempted suicide*
anxiety	*suicide*

Problems of regular heavy use

Sustained excessive consumption of alcohol gives rise to a variety of problems in addition to those related to intoxication.

A number of deiseases are recognised as particularly related to heavy alcohol use. These include:

cirrhosis of the liver	*fatty liver disease*
hepatitis	*diabetes*
circulatory system diseases	*brain damage*
peripheral neuritis	*gastritis*
cancer of the oesophagus	

Regular heavy drinking also gives rise to a range of other social, legal, physical and psychological problems including:

family problems	*fraud*
divorce	*debt*
homelessness	*vagrancy*
work difficulties	*habitual convictions for drunkenness*
unemployment	*financial difficulties*
obesity	*reactions with other drugs*
sexual dysfunction	*infertility*
nutritional deficiencies	*insomnia*
delirium tremens	*depression*
withdrawal fits	*anxiety*
hallucinosis	*attempted suicide*
dementia	*suicide*
gambling	*changes in personality*
misuse of other drugs	*amnesia*

Problems of dependence

This group is by far the best known. Such problems are commonly seen as the problems of 'alcoholics'. The idea of alcoholism as a disease argues that 'alcoholics' experience loss of control over drinking and an inability to refrain from drinking or, once drinking has begun, to stop it.

It is impossible to consider alcohol problems without some kind of exploration of what is meant by an 'alcohol problem' or 'alcoholism'. A counsellor's definition will determine who is and who is not identified as having a problem. Thus, in an extreme case, if someone believes that only spirit drinkers really have problems (as was commonly believed in the eighteenth century) people who drink beer will be ignored, probably to their detriment.

Throughout the last century efforts have been made to answer the question 'What is alcoholism?' The answers produced have ranged from viewing it as a moral failing to describing it as a medical syndrome. Yet no matter how the professional or the lay person describes the so-called 'alcoholic', the inference has been the same. The 'alcoholic' is an easily defined person who has a clear-cut and recognisable condition.

This condition has usually been defined by the drinker losing control over drinking. Once the drinker has taken one drink, drinking is bound to continue until oblivion is reached. This is the defining characteristic of the 'disease model' of 'alcoholism' propounded by Alcoholics Anonymous (AA). The 'alcoholic' has a recognised disease and the first step for any new AA member on the road to sobriety is admitting that the drinker is powerless over alcohol.

More recent terms such as 'Alcohol Dependence Syndrome' acknowledge both biological and psychological aspects of dependence. The question of the definition of terms like 'alcoholism' is explored below. Counsellors with such drinkers have identified several symptoms or 'dependence markers':
- withdrawal symptoms, e.g. anxiety, discomfort, shaking, due to the absence of the drug
- tolerance to alcohol
- less and less variation in drinking habits
- importance of drinking over other aspects of life
- relief drinking—to alleviate withdrawal symptoms
- thinking about alcohol to the exclusion of other thoughts
- return to original drinking patterns after abstinence
- craving for alcohol.

Dependent drinkers also suffer a range of psychological and social problems. Such as those listed above under intoxication and regular heavy consumption.

Occupations

It is also useful in identifying problem drinkers to recognise that certain occupations are considered 'high risk'. The most obvious professions would be:

- the licensed and catering trade where access to alcohol is so easy
- the Navy and Merchant Marine with its tradition of alcohol consumption.

However, a number of other work groups including journalists, the police and some those undertaking heavy industrial tasks all have above average rates of alcohol problems. Further information on this issue can be found in some of the reading in the bibliography.

A warning: misdiagnosis

So far this section has emphasised the danger of failing to recognise the problem drinkers in a caseload. It is worth pointing out the opposite problem—too readily assuming that alcohol is the problem. The following case study helps to make the point:

One older person, a Russian by birth, was taken to an accident and emergency unit after collapsing in the street. He was assessed as having fallen because he was drunk and was given a drug that both confused him and made him doubly incontinent. On returning to our hostel he was so confused that he urinated on his own furniture. His original fall was caused by a hardening of the arteries, not drink. He never touched drink as he was a very religious man.[7]

It is very easy with certain client groups, particularly the homeless, to assume too readily that alcohol is the problem. In the above case the consequences were potentially extremely serious, and serve to emphasise the need for careful assessment.

Withdrawals

People who drink heavily over a long period may find that they suffer withdrawal symptoms when they stop drinking. It is important to emphasise that this is not always the case. Only a minority of drinkers will experience such withdrawal symptoms. Of these, most will suffer shaking, sweating, nausea, and difficulty in sleeping. A few will experience more severe symptoms like the vivid hallucinations of delirium tremens or withdrawal fits. These latter symptoms are dangerous conditions and demand medical attention.

This is a very difficult area even for the experienced counsellor. Assessing the likelihood of withdrawal is essentially a medical skill. There are some indicators which can help the non-medical counsellor. Thus, the following people are more likely to experience withdrawal symptoms than other drinkers:
* those who have been drinking very heavily for a long time
* those who have had a binge of heavy drinking in the immediate past
* those who have a history of fits
* those who have had previous problems in withdrawing.

The client may well be the best judge of the likelihood of withdrawal, however if the counsellor has the slightest doubt the client should be referred to a General Practitioner.

HIV/AIDS

HIV / AIDS is recognisably associated in the public mind with injecting drug use. However, alcohol may also be a key factor in the spread of the virus. There is a reasonable likelihood that people, both heterosexual and homosexual, will be less sensible about practising safe sex when under the influence of alcohol.

There is also some evidence that heavy alcohol consumption may further weaken the immune system for people with HIV and thus hasten the advent of full-blown AIDS. This is particularly relevant to people who may be using alcohol to deal with the emotional trauma of being HIV positive.

Medication

Alcohol is a powerful drug. As such it can have a negative effect when mixed with certain prescribed drugs. The most obvious problem is with prescribed tranquillisers such as diazepam or lorazepam. Alcohol accentuates the effects of these drugs and will make the user very drunk. However, alcohol may effect a number of other drugs:
Central Nervous System Depressants, e.g. Barbiturates, Benzodiazepines, Anti-emetics and Pethidine. All these drugs have their effects enhanced, possibly dangerously so, when mixed with alcohol.

Aspirin: Alcohol and aspirin combined may cause gastrointestinal bleeding.

Oral Anticoagulants: e.g. Warfarin. Alcohol enhances the effects of these drugs.

Antidepressants: e.g. amitriptyline. Alcohol combined with these drugs will give a powerful sedative effect.

Alcohol also affects:
Antihypertensives, Anaesthetics, and other drugs.

This list is far from exhaustive—if in doubt, consult a doctor or pharmacist.

Good Practice for Counsellors Working
with Problem Drinkers

Who has an alcohol problem?

This booklet suggests the key to good practice lies in the counsellor's understanding of the nature of alcohol problems. This understanding will have an impact on:

- ensuring problem drinkers are identified
- ensuring alcohol problems are picked up earlier rather than later
- ensuring an appropriate range of treatment options are offered
- ensuring the special needs of particular groups such as older people are recognised.

This section focuses on exploring the nature of alcohol problems.

What type of model?

For many years AA was the most important, if not the only, organisation combating drink problems. It is therefore important to look at the limitations and alternatives to this approach.

While the work of AA has helped many people over the last fifty years, there are two serious drawbacks to this disease model:

1.   The theory is neither predictive nor preventative.
A car handbook that only recognises the type of breakdown that leaves a car lying in a heap by the side of the road is of little use in keeping a vehicle on the road. The tragedy of the 'disease model' is that it only allows the identification of alcohol-related problems when they are in their most extreme form, i.e. when all control has been lost over drinking, if not life. It is obvious that that way lies tragedy. One could neither hope to stop people moving towards a state of serious loss of control, nor recognise that people can have problems with alcohol without losing control. What is needed is a guide that pinpoints the earlier, if not smaller indicators that if corrected early, will prevent a full breakdown.

2.   The disease model is limited in the treatment options that it offers. Because the disease model only recognises problems in their extreme forms, its method of treatment is equally extreme, i.e. lifelong abstinence. Of course, for people whose drinking has become chaotic, abstinence may be the only option. If, however, we see a wider range of alcohol problems than the narrow view of the disease model reveals, is abstinence still the best option?

Before a counsellor recommends abstinence as the only viable alternative for all people experiencing drink related problems, it is important to be aware of the positive effects alcohol has for most people. It is also crucial that alcohol agencies are seen to be realistic— that the advice being dispensed can actually be carried out.

Is the young man with two drink-drive offences going to be interested in working with a counsellor that is saying 'abstinence is your only option'? It is far more likely that he will avoid it like the plague.

Is the older woman whose drinking problem is due to the fact that her pension is so small that even a slightly above average consumption of alcohol means she must eat less, going to be keen on abstinence? Is not reduced/controlled drinking a better option?

In the last fifteen years there has been a growing body of evidence that some form of controlled drinking is a viable alternative for many people. This is particularly true of less damaged clients with a shorter drinking history. For example, many older problem drinkers will fall into this category. A greater proportion of the general population will fall into it if we identify problems at an early stage.

It is unwise to recommend a drink-free future for someone if the only evidence for such a recommendation is based upon a theory produced at a time when the only way to explain alcohol problems was as an incurable disease. Professionals who impart knowledge and advice need to offer treatment options which are likely to be appropriate and perhaps more importantly, appealing, to a range of different needs.

So if the disease model is abandoned what can be put in its place? How does the counsellor decide who has a drinking problem and who does not?

What matters is that the new approach aids prevention and helps develop treatment options. The alternative is very simple.

Instead of a theory, or a set of signs and symptoms, or a recommended safe level of drinking, the guideline should be the question:

Is alcohol causing the person or those around him or her, any problems or difficulties?

The thrust of the intervention should be at the context in which drinking is taking place. What 'problems' are caused by the drinking?

By taking this approach we can look at the whole range of problems caused by alcohol:
* the counsellor is not limited to helping the extreme cases but can help anyone who is experiencing problems because of drinking.
* the counsellor does not adopt a disease model which can be seen as minimising the client's responsibility, indeed it emphasises that the difficulty is very much in the person's own hands.
* the counsellor will become aware of a much wider range of problems which will demand that counsellors offer a whole range of treatment options.

If this model is applied to case study situations and the needs of actual people, its usefulness becomes very apparent.

Case Studies

The stereotypical problem drinker has been drinking for a very long time, drinks a bottle of spirits each day, has suffered physical damage, leads a restricted life mainly spent drinking, has few social contacts, drinks instead of eating, lives in squalor, and above all doesn't want help.

However, if we look at some brief real life case studies we will see that the reality of problem drinking covers a much wider range of behaviours than the 'chronic drunk'.

Joginder is 65 and has just retired from a responsible job. He made few plans for his retirement and is now rather bored and lacking company. He has drunk socially for most of his life, but is now going to the pub more and more to fill his time and meet people. His wife is worried that he may be spending more on alcohol than they can afford.

Timothy is 21, unemployed, and married with a seven month old daughter. The only source of income is state benefit. Timothy spends most evenings at home, but likes to go down to a nearby pub every lunchtime and have a couple of pints with another unemployed friend. Susan, his wife, is very upset that Tim is spending nearly £20 per week on alcohol.

Carlton is 25. He went to the pub on Saturday lunchtime and had four pints of lager. Afterwards he and some friends took several cans back home to watch some videos. Later they went to another pub, played some pool and drank more lager. In the evening they went on to a party. Just as he was leaving, Carlton lost his balance and fell down the stairs, knocking himself out. He woke up in hospital with head injuries.

Frances is 19. She recently got a good job as a computer rep. She was especially pleased as a smart car went with the job. The day she got the job she went out to a club with some friends to celebrate. When they left the club there were no taxis to be found. Frances thought she would take a chance and drive home. 'This is the last time I'll be using this old banger' she thought. The police stopped Frances before she had got halfway home. She was fined. She also lost her driving licence and, of course, her new job.

Emily is in her 70's. She saw her parents, with whom she lived, die unexpectedly just before her retirement. On leaving work she shut the door on the world and began to drink and neglect herself.

Few of the people in these case studies fit the traditional stereotype of the heavy drinker/'alcoholic'. Yet all of them have alcohol-related problems, and all of them may need help to look at their drinking pattern and the effect alcohol is having on them. Counsellors need to be alive to the fact that people with drinking problems can be of many types.

If counsellors stick to the stereotyped image, the needs of many drinkers will be missed.

In a practical vein this approach solves a thorny problem. Many counsellors face people who say: 'all right I drink a bit, but I'm not an alcoholic'. The approach in this booklet says it doesn't matter whether the drinker describes him or herself as an 'alcoholic' or not. What matters is whether the drinking causes a problem. If there is a problem, the counsellor can then look at the ways of intervening outlined in a later chapter.

Good practice—the needs of particular groups

This book has emphasised that problem drinkers are a very disparate group of people with very varied needs. In this context it is important to examine the following:
- older people
- people from ethnic minorities
- men and women
- people with learning difficulties.

These are, of course, not the only groups which may need particular attention. Young people, the single homeless and gay and lesbian men and women may also have special needs when being helped with an alcohol problem.

Alcohol & older people

Many people are surprised by the idea that older people can experience alcohol problems. This is particularly the case since people over 65 are the group of adults who drink the least. Yet, alcohol can effect older people in exactly the same way as younger people. The statistics are misleading, the large number of older people who drink nothing or very little mask the problems of those who do drink. Some older people with alcohol problems will, of course, be people who have drunk heavily for many years and have simply grown old with their problem. However some aspects of old age mean that older people will be harmed in certain additional ways.

Counsellors should consider the following issues when working with older problem drinkers:

1. Accidents:
Alcohol impairs co-ordination thus creating the risk of accidents. In an older person whose co-ordination may already be poor the likelihood of accidents is that much greater. In particular, alcohol can exacerbate tremulousness of the hands. Poor concentration due to alcohol can also lead to accidents. If a person has, for example brittle bones the consequences of these falls could be very serious.

2.   Depression:
     Alcohol is a depressant drug. It is not a stimulant. It depresses the central nervous system. As a result drinking can cause or exacerbate an existing state of depression. In particular, this may be the result of one of the many circumstances surrounding 'loss'.

3.   Hypothermia:
     Contrary to the popular belief alcohol does not warm people up. It actually makes them colder. Older people who drink to keep warm are, therefore, running the risk of hypothermia.

4.   Poor nutrition:
     Alcohol is not a good source of nourishment. It contains calories but little else. Moreover, alcohol can also effect people's digestion and can lead as a result to poor nutrition. Older people who find it hard to prepare their own meals have been known to use alcohol as a substitute food.

5.   Financial Problems:
     Many older people find themselves on an increasingly limited income. Alcohol is inevitably a drain on a small income. Conversely there is a growing group of people who are retiring with a reasonable income and are finding they have little to occupy them than alcohol.

6.   Incontinence:
     Alcohol can increase the likelihood of loss of control of bowel and bladder movements.

7.   Poor relationships:
     Alcohol can increase tension in relationships. This may lead on occasions to physical violence as exampled by cases of 'elder abuse'[9]. At the very least, drinking may increase the isolation of already lonely people.

8.   Poor memory:
     Alcohol can diminish the power to remember things, especially recent events. Thus alcohol may aggravate a process already present in many older people.

9.   Mixing drugs and alcohol:
     The problems of mixing alcohol with other drugs has already been mentioned. Many older people are taking some form of prescribed medication. Some may be taking a whole cocktail of different drugs. Drinking alcohol on top of any drug is always something to be considered carefully, but when a whole variety of different drugs is being consumed it is almost certainly going to lead to problems.

10. The possibility of misdiagnosis:
This problem was mentioned above, but it is particularly acute with older people. There are cases of older people with distinct hand tremors being diagnosed as having Parkinson's Disease, when in reality the shakiness was caused by alcohol withdrawals. In addition, Parkinsonian drugs mix very badly with alcohol.

However, the problem of misdiagnosis is not restricted to Parkinson's disease. One of the problems of alcohol abuse amongst older people is that those symptoms which are commonly (although often wrongly) seen as the effects of old age and those of alcohol use can be very similar. Poor memory, failing co-ordination, incontinence, accidents, depression and shakiness can all be associated with either ageing or alcohol. A healthy but intoxicated person could be assessed as suffering prematurely from the ageing process.

Different effects of alcohol on men and women

On average men drink more alcohol than women, and although it does not necessarily follow, it seems that men are more likely to have an alcohol problem than women. Most alcohol agencies see more male than female clients, however some anecdotal and statistical evidence suggests that the proportion of women to men is steadily increasing.

Physical Differences
The simple difference in average size between men and women means that the same quantity of alcohol is likely to have more effect on a woman than a man. However, because women tend to have less fluid in their body than men and more fats in their bloodstream (which slows the rate at which alcohol is absorbed) even a large woman is likely to experience more harm from drinking than a similar sized man. This means that women are more prone to physical damage such as liver cirrhosis than men. Thus, the safe levels for women's drinking are lower than men's (14 units per week against 21 units).

Physical differences can raise a number of other issues:
1. Drinking can cause impotence in men, and this may be a concern for a considerable number of clients. The notion that men should be 'macho' may make it particularly difficult to talk about.

2. Pregnant women must consider the possibility of the Foetal Alcohol Syndrome. Drinking can cause physical and mental harm to the foetus. It is not clear what level of drinking will cause this, it is therefore recommended that pregnant women avoid alcohol.
3. Pre-menstrual tension and the menopause may be reasons for women increasing their drinking.
4. Because females mature earlier than males it may be that early teenage drinking is more a female than a male phenomenon.
5. Women tend to live longer than men therefore older people's drinking is more of a female issue.

Social Differences

Social attitudes effect the way men and women drink. It is still less acceptable for women to drink, especially in certain situations e.g. alone in a pub, and even more unacceptable for a woman to be drunk than for a man. While these attitudes may be changing it still means that a woman with a drink problem will be more stigmatised than a man. This may mean that women will conceal their drinking and consequent problems. On the other hand it may be that because women's drinking is less tolerated than a man's they will recognise their problem earlier than men.

Social differences also have the effect of encouraging men to drink . Heavy drinking is seen as a way of proving a man's masculinity, if not of making a man more sexually attractive. Advertising in the media can encourage this image building. However, advertisers are now encouraging females to see drinking as part of being an exciting young woman.

Situational differences

Other differences will depend more on the types of situation in which men and women are likely to find themselves rather than any innate difference. For example:
*   women are more likely to find themselves in the position of being left at home after the children have gone their own ways and feeling their life is empty and unfulfilled.
*   men are more likely to centre their social lives around a heavy drinking culture such as a pub or club.
*   men are still more likely to be in jobs where heavy drinking seems to be the norm, but this may be changing.

- men and women are likely to buy their drink in different places. Women are more likely to buy it in supermarkets and drink it at home, whereas men are more likely to buy and drink it in a pub or club.
- because of G.P. prescribing practices, women are more likely to mix alcohol with tranquillisers such as lorazepam.

All these factors need to be taken into consideration as the helping process develops. As in all counselling, consideration will have to be given to the sex of the counsellor. While some people will happily see a counsellor of either sex, a choice ought to be available.

People from ethnic minorities

People from ethnic minorities are clearly not a homogenous group. The problems of the person from a Muslim family where alcohol consumption is totally banned are going to be very different from someone of a West Indian or Jewish background.

At the moment research into the varying nature of alcohol problems among ethnic communities is very poor. Even anecdotal evidence is contradictory–some suggesting that ethnic communities have considerable numbers of alcohol problems, others that this is a small and insignificant problem.

Counsellors must keep an open mind and be alert to the possibility of alcohol problems in any group.

People with learning difficulties

In the last few years and, in particular, with the growth of community care alcohol agencies have become aware of a number of people with learning difficulties who have experienced problems with alcohol. The following case study serves to highlight the problem:

Robert is a 34 year old man with learning difficulties. He has lived his life between his parents and a variety of institutions. His father was a heavy drinker who frequently beat his mother. Robert often drank heavily when at home, but drank little in the large specialist hospital where he lived until recently. Last year he moved into a small community home. He shares this house with several other residents and there is a staff team to support them.

Shortly after moving in, Robert began to drink heavily on a regular but not continual basis. These drinking bouts would be accompanied by verbal abuse to people in and out of the house and sometimes threats of violence.

The staff tried reasoning, cajoling and persuasion to try and encourage Robert to change his drinking. However, all these efforts failed. Finally the staff decided to put Robert under threat of dismissal. If he drank again he would have to return to the Hospital. This had the desired effect. Robert stopped drinking.

Unfortunately the staff now face a dilemma. Robert appears to be under control in the house, but what will happen when he moves into his own accommodation? Because he is being forced not to drink, he isn't learning anything about dealing with alcohol. What will happen if that control is removed?

This book cannot offer any detailed guidance on working with this specific client group. However, it is clear that a specialist area like this will demand a team approach involving both those with knowledge about learning difficulties and alcohol counsellors.

Issues Arising for Counsellors

Counsellors are likely to encounter problem drinkers on their caseloads in one of two ways:
- clients coming directly for help with an alcohol problem
- clients coming for another reason but for whom alcohol emerges as a significant underlying problem.

For the majority of counsellors whose work does not focus on alcohol problems the latter is likely to be the most common occurrence. This section looks at the following:
- the problems of raising the issue of drinking with clients
- simple ways of working with problem drinkers
- longer term counselling.

Raising the issue

The earlier chapters have shown that identifying a problem drinker does not have to be a great problem. If a counsellor stays alert to the possibility that drink could be involved for any client, then examples of alcohol problems will soon become apparent.

However, identifying a client is one thing, talking about it is something else entirely. It seems that many caring professionals find it hard to broach the subject of a client's drinking. Even in role play situations there often seems to be a barrier between recognition and discussion. This is not simply because it is difficult to phrase an appropriate opening. A counsellor may experience a range of anxieties about tackling a client e.g.

1. Will the client respond with physical or verbal abuse?
2. Will broaching the subject ruin the relationship?
3. Will the counsellor feel embarrassed about talking about a client's drinking?
4. Will the counsellor know what to do if the client does want help?
5. Will it mean more work?
6. Will the client deny it completely?
7. Is it really important to talk about alcohol problems?
8. Does the counsellor believe that nothing can be done for problem drinkers anyway?

It would be easy to dismiss such fears as unfounded and ridiculous. As one reads through them some are obviously poor reasons for not talking to the client. For example, there are clearly possibilities for change with such clients and a competent counsellor should at least know how to find out where suitable help might be available. However, anxieties about ruining the relationship, feeling embarrassed, or facing abuse, are harder to dismiss. Such anxieties are dependent on the personalities of the two people and the nature of their relationship.

Although these anxieties may be real, they are not reasons for avoiding the issue. Instead counsellors need to take steps to tackle the issue as best they can. They need to acknowledge that working with some clients can make them feel uneasy, but nonetheless deal with their problems. If these feelings remain unacknowledged, it is likely that almost unconsciously the counsellor will avoid the unpleasant issues.

These points may seem obvious, but there is an immense amount of evidence that caring professionals do not work with problem drinkers even though there may be many such clients on their caseload. Counsellors need to be rigorous in asking themselves if they are identifying and tackling problem drinkers.

Denial

The most common frustration in working with such clients is the issue of denial. Undoubtedly the likelihood of denial is minimised if questions are asked appropriately (see later section), but all the same, some clients will deny that alcohol is a problem even if the evidence is staring them in the face. This can seem very negative to the counsellor involved, the effort seems to have been wasted and there is little incentive to tackle other clients.

This attitude has to be turned on its head. Denial is not a negative process. It may show that this client is not prepared at the moment, to talk about the issue of drinking with that counsellor, but that does not make the approach a waste of effort.

A client who denies a problem, has almost certainly heard what was said. It may not be acknowledged, but the more firmly something is denied the more likely it is that it has hit home. It is the experience of many alcohol agencies that they will see clients who have denied their drinking to other workers but finally admit it to a specialist service. The earlier workers have done a good job in planting a seed in the client's mind, it is just frustrating that they never see it come to fruition.

There are, thus, four key points to bear in mind about tackling denial:

1. The likelihood of denial is diminished by using the right language. Words are important and their impact should be considered carefully.

2. Some people will find it hard to open up unless the topic is broached for them.

Third and most crucial:

3. **Denial is not negative**. Just because the client says, 'You're wrong!' doesn't mean the message hasn't been heard. Indeed the more adamant the denial, the more certain one can be that the message has hit home. Denial does not mean that the worker's efforts have been wasted. Instead it simply means that that person isn't ready to open up about the drinking yet. The counsellor should see the comment as a seed that may not bear fruit now, but could do later. Frustratingly enough for the counsellor it may be that the person opens up to someone else entirely.

Finally:

4. Even if saying something never has any effect on a particular person, at least the counsellor has offered the option to change. Thus it is vital that if drink is causing a client problems, someone, if not a number of people must say something about it. To do otherwise is to collude with and encourage the drinking. The more people that make the point the more likely it is that change will occur. If nothing is said, then the counsellor is giving the message that all is well with the client's drinking. This is surely the minimum responsibility that counsellors have to those they are helping–offering them alternatives.

Saying something

The effect of any comment will, of course, depend on the way the comment is framed and counsellors must think carefully about what they say. Most statements will force the client to do some thinking about drinking, however some comments will be more helpful than others.

The most helpful comments will have three characteristics. They will be:
a) Non-threatening
b) Specific and personal
c) Made when the client is sober.

a)   **Non-threatening:**
If a counsellor challenges a client by saying out of the blue–'I think you're an alcoholic', it will probably elicit an appropriate response, i.e. abuse, resentment, denial or at least a quick end to the conversation. The comment sounds like an accusation and uses a term–'alcoholic'– that has developed a distinctly pejorative overtone. While a drinker may hear such a comment, human desire to save face will probably lead to complete denial.

This is an extreme example, but it is very easy, either by word, expression, or attitude to convey a derogatory attitude to the problem drinker. In some cases these attitudes may actually reflect a person's feelings about the client but neither the client nor the counsellor will be helped if those attitudes spill over into the conversation.

A much better introduction would be a less accusatory approach such as:

'Have you ever thought that drink may be causing you problems?' or

'Do you think drink could be contributing to the problems you are experiencing?'

Such openings as these are neither judgemental nor using loaded terms. They are thus less likely to be perceived as threatening by the drinker and to elicit an unwanted response.

b)   **Being specific and personal:**
Open and non-threatening questions may not always produce an admission of anxiety about the drinking. The client may still find it too dangerous to open up, or may genuinely not see things the way the counsellor perceives them. In such cases counsellors will probably not find it helpful to keep on badgering away trying to encourage or force the client to admit the problem. Instead the focus of the intervention should be changed from the client's problem to the problems the counsellor is having because of the drinker's behaviour.

It is ultimately impossible to prove to an unwilling client that a problem exists. There is no scientific test, no litmus paper which can turn up a solid and irrefutable result. Thus any comment which begins: 'You must have a problem/ be an alcoholic because you do x,y, or z. . . ' is doomed to failure. The client can always respond by saying something like: 'I'm not a problem drinker because I don't sit on a park bench and drink meths.' or 'It's not a problem because I don't think it's a problem'. Such comments are indisputable.

c)   **Made when the client is sober:**
The strategies above, as well as any other efforts at changing behaviour are best made when the client is sober. This point is obvious and basic, but often ignored. The moment at which a counsellor is most likely to both recognise and want to do something about a drinking problem is when the client is drunk. When the client is sober the need to say something may seem less pressing.

It is unlikely that anything useful will be achieved by talking with someone who is drunk. The client may not even remember what was said let alone take seriously any promises that were made. The counsellor would be better advised to take time to sit and talk when the person is sober.

Counsellors may claim that finding a moment when the client is sober is exactly the problem. There is a strong myth that problem drinkers are always drunk. This is not true. Most clients will have periods, albeit short in some cases, when they are sober. Even the seemingly most 'inveterate drunk' can usually sober up to some extent for a period if asked.

If a counsellor shows that sobriety really is expected, then clients will comply. This may mean that the client who is asked to sober up for an appointment but who still arrives drunk, will have to be shown quite clearly that drunkenness is not acceptable and the interview terminated. If a counsellor refuses to collude, by talking to the client drunk when they asked for sobriety, the client will often comply.

Simple ways of working with problem drinkers

The process of changing behaviour

Helping people with alcohol problems is essentially about encouraging change it is therefore important that counsellors understand the process of change. This book offers one model for understanding how people change. This is not the only model, but is one that is particularly appropriate to working with alcohol problems.

The cycle of change: a comprehensive model

When people try to change a piece of behaviour – especially if it is something that has been going on for a long time – they will go through more or less the same process. This tends to be a pattern of:
* going through a period of considering the change before taking action
* failing
* trying again until . . .
* finally succeeding (hopefully!)

To clarify this point it is worth thinking of a personal behaviour that the reader has changed, e.g. moving house, losing weight, giving up smoking. The process will be very similar. This point is worth making to illustrate that changes made by problem drinkers are not totally different from the changes that other people make. Therefore, the counsellor may have some personal experience to draw on in counselling.

The idea that behavioural change involves several changes was developed by J.O. Prochaska and C.C. DiClemente[10] into a four stage cyclical model. This is shown on the next page. According to the model successful change involves four stages:

Contemplation—wondering if there's a need to change behaviour
Action—deciding to change behaviour and doing something about it
Maintenance—'staying changed', involving a gradual decrease in desire to return to the original behaviour
Relapse—a return to the original behaviour.

NB: Before achieving successful long-term change, most people relapse. The vast majority of relapsers move back into contemplation and continue the cycle. Many people relapse several times..

There are two further stages associated with the cycle of change:

Pre-contemplation—before someone is aware that a problem exists. The cycle of change is entered from this stage with the contemplation stage coming next.

Termination—when the problem no longer exists.
This is reached from the maintenance stage. Successful changers leave the cycle of change and 'terminate the addiction'. Some leave the cycle and return to a dependent life style. Some get blocked at various stages e.g. unable to move from contemplation to action, or action to maintenance. Some never feel free of the risk of relapse and remain in the maintenance stage.

An understanding of this model helps the counsellor to identify the needs of the client more accurately. For example, there is no point attempting to introduce strategies for reducing drinking if the client is in the pre-contemplation stage.

THE STAGES OF CHANGE
Prochaska & Di Clementi

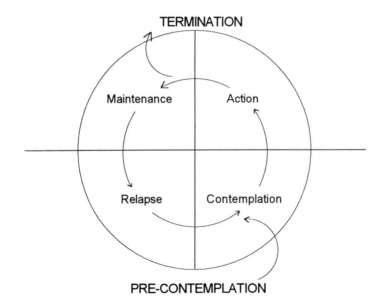

Simple Interventions with Problem Drinkers

> '. . . it is only when we professionals can reduce our irrational wish to do such a good and complete piece of work that the client will never again need help that we can begin to see what limited but worthwhile intervention is possible.'[11]

Counsellors, like all care workers, sometimes have unrealistic expectations of what they, and their clients, can achieve. It is important that those working with problem drinkers do not feel they have failed if:
* they do not 'cure' the clients instantly
* the clients do not keep to agreed targets
* the clients give up on counselling

It is vital that counsellors remember one basic point:
Only the drinker can change the drinking behaviour–the counsellor cannot 'cure' the client.

Unless this is kept firmly in mind, the counsellor may face great discouragement and frustration; ultimately the ability to work with such clients will be impaired. The next sections focus on simple things that counsellors can do to help problem drinkers.

Identify early

Prevention is always better than cure. If a drink problem can be tackled in its early stages then that will save much trouble and effort later on.

Of course, this is of little comfort to the counsellor facing someone whose drinking is already causing serious problems. However, it is important that individual counsellors and agencies alike learn from current experience and recognise the value of doing something earlier rather than later.

Early identification might entail any one of a number of measures, for example:

a) **Asking about drinking problems as a routine.**
Many agencies will be in the position of regularly assessing the needs of a client group e.g. older people. Some agencies have set themselves the task of asking all those they assess about their drinking. They have usually been surprised by the number of positive replies they receive and the needs they reveal. Workers often feel reluctant to take this on. Drinking is still a taboo subject for many people, but the anxieties are more often on the counsellors side than the client's. It is down to the counsellors to overcome these difficulties.

b) **Keeping one's eyes open for drinking problems.**
Alcohol problems are common, if counsellors keep their eyes open for them, they will see them. If they wait until the drinking sticks out a mile, it will be necessary to intervene when the problem is at its worst.

Saying something

There is one element which is common to any attempt to change someone's drinking–'Say something about the problem.' Space has already been devoted to this issue above. It is worth re-emphasising certain points.

By recognising a problem but not saying anything, the counsellor is helping the drinker to carry on drinking. If there is no challenge to the behaviour, the client is given the message that the drinking is acceptable.

The aim of saying something is to:
a) Make the person aware of your perception of their drinking.
b) Give the person the opportunity to open up and seek help.

As has been said, this does not mean badgering the client into admitting a problem. The intention is to say something short, simple and to the point about the counsellor's perception of the drinking. It also implies saying it at a suitable moment and in an appropriate manner.

Giving information

The next stage in the helping process is the simple provision of information. The kind of information will fall into two types:

a)   If help is wanted—the information may simply be the whereabouts of alcohol counselling, or putting the person in touch with such help if unable to make contact alone.

b)   If help isn't wanted, then the counsellor should, at least, give information on the physical/social effects of alcohol. The giving of advice and education should not be under-rated. There are many people who may be doing themselves harm for all the reasons mentioned above despite drinking quite small amounts. These people may be helped with a little advice and information.

The person may well not want the information, or be shy about appearing to want the information. This will make it difficult to give verbally. If so, pamphlets are a good alternative. There are now a range of these available from health promotion units or local alcohol advice agencies. It is a good idea to seek out such leaflets before they are needed so that they are to hand when the moment comes.

The material available earlier in the book can be drawn on as a source of advice and useful information.

Talking to the family

It should never be forgotten that the family of a problem drinker may need help as much as the drinker. Alongside the obvious problems of physical or emotional abuse and neglect, family members may carry a great burden of unexpressed feelings. These may range from a sense that they are somehow to blame for the drinker's behaviour to an enormous and unexpressed anger about the situation. A counsellor can help a family simply by allowing the space to express these emotions and reassuring them about their role in the matter.

Families are, of course, very complex systems and helping the non-drinking partner may force the drinker to change behaviour. Thus if a wife stops colluding with her husband's drinking by buying him alcohol, he will be forced to behave differently.

To initiate such changes will demand broaching the topic with the family. This may be just as difficult as talking to the drinker. The family may be very skilled at concealing the nature of their home life, or long ago given up talking about the drinker's behaviour. To break down these barriers, a counsellor will need to use the same skills and methods that were outlined above.

Encouraging change

Having helped the client reach the point where help is sought, is an excellent piece of work in itself. The counsellor does not need to go further. The next stage in the helping process could be done by someone else, perhaps a specialist substance abuse agency. At the back of this book there is a list of addresses that can be referred to for advice on local help. That said, the helper can continue the helping process if s/he so wishes.

Below are offered some very simple techniques to help the drinker think about changing her drinking.

Introduction

Major hurdles in helping problem drinkers are client compliance and overcoming workers' anxieties about such work. If these two barriers are surmounted, the task is straightforward enough to be carried out by any counsellor. If a client is asking for help, and the counsellor feels confident enough to provide help there should be few problems.

However, two caveats should be entered:

- in some situations, e.g. working with older people or mothers with children, a multidisciplinary approach may be most helpful. Thus with the older person, local day care, nursing and befriending services may be useful. Counsellors need to remain open to the possibility of multi-disciplinary work.

- if a case is very complex counsellors could look to a specialist agency for help. However, this does not have to be a simple referral on, but could rather be joint work between the two agencies.

Providing help

Counsellors will work in a variety different styles with their clients. It would, therefore, be clearly pointless to tell counsellors how to undertake long term counselling with a problem drinker. This work will be no different from long term work with any other client and will be pursued as the counsellor's personal style and the clients wishes, dictate. This section concentrates instead, on the more mechanical aspects of counselling someone to change the actual drinking behaviour. Most counsellors will find it helpful to use some behavioural techniques for this part of the process. After that counsellors will pursue their own style to resolve the issues that have caused the drink problem.

The first step is to discover in what ways the client wants to change the drinking. There are two basic options: total abstinence or controlled drinking

As a general rule the younger, healthier, less damaged by alcohol, more personally supported and more socially established a client is, the more likely the client will be to be able to control the drinking.

This is not an absolute rule but a guide to likely success. Ultimately, the client will always make the choice. If an older and damaged client insists on choosing controlled drinking it may be best to begin working with that rather than force the client into an unwanted abstinence. Only in cases where continued drinking is likely to result in serious harm e.g. where there is liver damage, might the counsellor refuse to consider controlled drinking.

Total Abstinence
Before a client gives up alcohol, the possibility of withdrawals should be considered. By and large withdrawals will not extend beyond shakiness, sweats, poor sleep and a disturbed appetite, and can be overcome in a few days with rest, relaxation and friendly support.

Useful practical advice at this time is to encourage the client to take vitamins especially B6; not to worry if sleep is difficult – it will return to normal in a few weeks and to try and eat normally, even if not particularly hungry.

NB: It is worth remembering that tea and coffee also disturb sleep, some clients will turn to drinking large quantities of these drinks when they have given up alcohol. Of course, in the short term it will be too much to try and change this behaviour as well, however, caffeine's effects on sleep are worth bearing in mind in the longer term

If a client has a history of delirium tremens, or withdrawal fits it will be best to seek medical help as these can be dangerous. However, these are very rare conditions and counsellors should probably be more concerned about calming clients' unnecessary fears about withdrawal rather than any real harm to the client.

Controlled Drinking
Once client and counsellor have decided on a desired level of drinking, this can be achieved in one of three ways:

- a period of total abstinence, perhaps four weeks or more, followed by a gradual return to controlled drinking at the desired level. This is probably the preferred method, but entails the problem of withdrawals.

- a series of large cuts in weekly consumption until the desired level is reached. This is probably the least favoured of the methods and may entail withdrawals if the cuts are large enough.

- a series of small cuts in weekly intake. This can be a slow process, but has the advantage of boosting confidence after each small cut.

Throughout all this work, setting targets and monitoring their achievement will be the main theme. Each week a drinking target will be set–perhaps in terms of quantity drunk, or in terms of situations it is drunk in, and alongside this other targets will be set.

Drink Diaries
All the controlled drinking techniques will involve the use of a drink diary. This is a simple technique for monitoring whether a client has fulfilled a drinking target for the week. These diaries can also be used for a couple of weeks prior to setting a drinking goal to see how much and in what circumstances the client is actually drinking. The use of the drink diary is discussed later.

Not achieving the target

If a client does not achieve the drink target for a particular week it is not a calamity. It is nothing more or less than not achieving a fairly arbitrary target. It is only a disaster if counsellor and client believe it to be a disaster.

Counsellors should be positive rather than negative in such a situation. The client may still have drunk less than for a long time, and this should be emphasised. Even if drinking has stayed the same or increased, the client can still start again next week. Counsellors will facilitate this by showing confidence in the client.

Nor should a client switch from control to abstinence or vice-versa after just one week's effort. To switch swiftly would encourage a sense of failure.

Of course some client may not be making a serious effort to change. If, after a few weeks, this becomes obvious counsellors may feel it appropriate to point out that this is an unacceptable use of the counsellor's and the client's time.

Continued work

Over the first few weeks of sobriety or control, the task of setting targets and monitoring their achievement must continue, with the drinking targets increasingly being complemented by other goals. Much of this effort will be in the area of social skills that counsellors explore with other clients such as assertion skills, building relationships, or sorting out finances.

Similarly for many problem drinkers emotions are a key area of work. A client may be drinking because of an inability to deal with feelings like anger or love. Once sober the client may face feelings of guilt, fear or anxiety connected to past or future behaviour. The counsellor will need to explore these issues and help the client find ways of dealing with such feelings, as would be the case with any other client.

Simple behavioural techniques for creating change

The simplest way to find out if a person is drinking over the safe limits is to ask the client to keep a diary. A blank diary can be found on page 49. (If poor literacy skills or disability make this difficult, a counsellor can go through the week's drinking verbally). The drinking is translated into units and the total then calculated and compared with the safe limits.

The diary has certain advantages:
* Simply using it on a daily basis can modify the drinking. Keeping a record is a good way of reducing drinking.
* It reveals to the drinker exactly how much she is drinking. Perhaps this will be the first time this has been seen so clearly.
* It points up particular points in a week that are most likely to lead to heavy or problematic drinking.
* If someone is trying to change, it offers a good record of progress.
* It shows the helper how much is being drunk.
* It highlights any pattern to the drinking.

Do people lie on diaries?
As a general rule–no. People will either fill it in accurately or 'forget' to do it. To sit down and forge a diary is a tremendous admission to oneself that something is wrong. The exception to this would be if some reward or punishment were riding on the outcome of the diary.

The first time that the diary is filled in, it should be nothing more than a record of behaviour. It is only in later weeks that there is a need to think about cutting down.

Tips for making drinking safer

Clients may also be helped by considering a few practical tips for reducing consumption of, or the harm from drinking. The following are a sample of the types of advice that might be offered:

1.   Eating while one drinks is the most obvious way of making any drinking safer. The food slows down the rate at which the alcohol passes into the bloodstream. Therefore, one becomes intoxicated more slowly. However, eating salty foods such as crisps, peanuts, or cheese are likely to make one more thirsty.

2.   Try drinking halves instead of pints. This may help in slowing down the rate of consumption.

3.   Start drinking later and stop drinking earlier in the day. In this way one can set one's own limits to the amount drunk.

4.   While out drinking, alone or with friends, try alternating soft drinks with alcoholic ones. Tonic water or shandy can look like alcohol. Of course, many pubs now also serve coffee.

5.   Avoid becoming part of a round. This will almost always increase the pressure to drink more.

6.   Be careful of the high alcohol lagers. These are much stronger than ordinary beer and will, thus, cause problems sooner.

An alternative starting point to the diary is with THE GOOD AND BAD THINGS ABOUT MY DRINKING (see Appendix 1):

This has a couple of useful features:
* It allows someone to make an objective decision about whether to change or not.
* It allows the helper and the person to see the advantages as well as the disadvantages of continued use.

It can, therefore, be useful in provoking thought on the part of the client as well as possibly highlighting some of the key issues involved.

There is more to working with a drinker than just changing the alcohol consumption. It is usually necessary to change at least some elements of a person's lifestyle. The size of the changes needed will depend on the extent of the drinking in the person's life. For example, if drinking in pubs is a person's entire social life, then finding an alternative lifestyle is going to be essential. This will demand looking at alternative social activities, setting goals in this area and examining rewards for achieving the target. The other behavioural sheets attached provide a way of exploring these issues.

Sheets 1 & 2:
Situations I find it harder/easier to avoid drink in
These first two sheets help determine what areas of a person's life need changing. They can be used alongside the diary and positive/negative sheet which also offer insights into areas for change.

Thus in the sample situations sheet the person has highlighted boredom as a key reason for drinking. The alternatives and situations sheets highlights going out and meeting people as a possible alternative behaviour. Thus when setting a task for the coming week on the goals sheet, joining a local day centre has been set as the target. The reward has been set as a visit to the local shopping centre.

Sheet 3: Goals & Rewards

Goals and rewards are vital. The older person needs clear targets and the helper something to check on. It is, therefore, important that both goal and reward is realistic and achievable. Thus a goal like 'I want to be nicer next week' is useless. Such a target is unreachable and uncheckable.

This pattern of goal and reward can continue until both parties are happy with the changed situation.

It is worth returning again to the point that the helper does not have to take on this process. Some situations may be so difficult that outside expertise is essential. There is no failure in asking for help, failure lies in not initiating the process at the very beginning.

Supporting colleagues

A great deal of energy is spent thinking about how the client can be helped to change. However, it is often the counsellors who need help. The following case study offers one example of the stresses of working with this client group:

Case Study

Kathryn worked as a counsellor in a small community based unit for ex-street drinkers. The house was home to a number of men in their fifties who had been re-housed from larger 'doss houses'.

The residents were allowed to drink. However one of them was increasingly allowing his drinking to get out of control. When under the influence of alcohol he became abusive and began to have paranoid fantasies about the staff members and other residents.

Kathryn felt very unhappy in this situation, she no longer enjoyed going into work. She was occasionally scared of what would happen. She felt she was no longer any good at her job and was in a spiral of depression about the situation.

On one occasion she likened this threatening situation to that of 'the daughter of a heavy drinker, experiencing emotional if not physical abuse'.

Problem drinkers can cause a great deal of distress. It is essential that the need to give emotional support to counsellors tackling this problem is recognised. For example, the counsellor may feel that it is a sign of weakness that no progress has been in achieved in changing a client's drinking.

Alcohol agencies will be happy to offer support to staff members and can help talk through strategies for change.

Dealing with intoxication

One of the inherent problems of working with problem drinkers is that some of the clients will occasionally arrive drunk. There is no single way of dealing with a drunk. The action taken will depend on the 'threat' posed by the person.

If the 'threat' is simply noise and disruption—the priority will be to get the drunk out of the building or at least out of the main work area.

If the 'threat' is violence to the counsellor or to other people-the priority will be to protect people.

If the main threat is to the drunk him or herself, i.e. danger of accident or injury—the priority will be to keep the drunk in a safe place until a relative or guardian can be called.

These points are essential. If a counsellor tries to evict a violent drunk rather than giving protection highest priority, dangerous consequences could result.

The following points offer some further guidance on handling drunkenness:

1. It may seem useful to know how a client behaves when drunk and to know what s/he talks about at this time, but it is usually a pointless exercise.
2. Most alcohol agencies only see sober clients or perhaps on a first occasion when slightly intoxicated. Some people have a tolerance for large amounts of alcohol. It is possible to go through a lengthy interview with an apparently mildly intoxicated client, only to find nothing is recalled afterwards. An interview with an intoxicated client is usually fruitless.
3. A client will welcome a safe place where it is clear that only sober people will be encountered. If there is a reasonable but high expectation of a client it is likely that that expectation will be met.
4. Even the most severe drinker is not drunk all the time and most will turn up sober to see a counsellor without needing to be asked. In fact drunkenness should be an exception.
5. If a client does turn up drunk, do not get into an argument. Make another appointment as soon as possible and ask the client to come sober. Be kind and firm and lead the client to the door.
6. In the rare event that a client is difficult or threatening or violent, remember:-
   a) women are often better at handling drunken people than men – they tend to invite less violence.
   b) If things look difficult – sitting down may diffuse the situation.
   c) Keep exits clear – don't let the drunk feel penned in. The counsellor may want an escape route too.

d) Keep the drunken in a reception area if possible and try not to take the client up or downstairs in case of accidents

e) Sometimes it is necessary to call the police.

7. When a client's relatives telephone and complain of violence in the home, they should be advised to call the police immediately.

However, as a general rule counsellors should insist that a client should come sober and do nothing more than make another appointment if someone does turn up drunk.

Training

There are now numerous training courses on working with problem drinkers. These range from university based diplomas to one day course run by local alcohol services. Alcohol Concern, the national agency on alcohol misuse, can advise on the most suitable courses.

Services for the Problem Drinker

There is now a network of general services which can offer varying degrees of assistance and different kinds of intervention to people with alcohol problems, the family members, and professional carers.

The services that exist fall into the following main groups:
Alcoholics Anonymous is the oldest and best known service. It is a pure self-help group for drinkers. AA works on the following principles:
- it involves groupwork
- it demands total abstinence as a solution to alcohol problems
- it has a solid programme which members work through
- it has a spiritual element to its approach.

AA has helped numerous clients but others find its approach inappropriate or unhelpful. In particular some clients may want individual counselling in a convenient location rather than groupwork.

Al-Anon and Al-Ateen are sister organisations of AA for family members and teenage children of drinkers respectively. They work on a very similar basis to AA.

Alcohol Treatment Units
are usually in-patient, hospital units providing detoxification and a short groupwork programme. They are a limited resource and often have waiting lists. Some units may give priority to younger clients. They also tend to concentrate on abstinence.

Alcohol Counselling
is offered either by voluntary organisations such as Alcohol Advisory Services or statutory community alcohol teams. The counselling will be one to one and some services may offer appointments in the clients home. They will offer a choice of either abstinence or controlled drinking and will also offer support or counselling to the family of clients. Counsellors could also turn to these services for support for themselves.

Day Centres/Residential Rehabilitation

Most are primarily aimed at homeless problem drinkers. The residential facilities will mainly target clients over 18 and under 65 years of age and will be abstinence orientated. Day centres will welcome any clients, but are few and far between, usually being found in city centres.

The best way to learn about these services is to visit them and see what they can offer. If in doubt about who to contact, start with the alcohol counselling or advisory services. They can point out the best service for a particular client.

Further help

There are many local services offering advice about alcohol problems. The best way to discover the nearest agency is to contact Alcohol Concern or one of the other national alcohol agencies. They can provide details of appropriate local help anywhere in the country. These agencies are listed in the next section.

Specialist services are also usually willing to offer you their support and experience of working with this client group.

Appendix 1—Check Sheets

Drinking Diary

	Morning	Qty	Afternoon	Qty	Evening	Qty
Monday						
Tuesday						
Wednesday						
Thursday						
Friday						
Saturday						
Sunday						

Target				Total	

The Good and the Bad Things about my Drinking

	What are the good things about my drinking?	What are the bad things about my drinking?
1.		
2.		
3.		
4.		
5.		
6.		
7.		
8.		
9.		
10.		

Now ask yourself: Do I want to change the way I drink?

Situations I find it harder/easier to avoid drink in

Situations in which I find it hard to avoid having a drink	Situations in which I find it easy to avoid having a drink

Have a look at your drinking diary when you do this.
Now: Can you swap any of the easy situations for the hard ones?

Goals and Rewards

My drinking goal this week is: .... **units**

What I will change this week:

How will I reward myself if I succeed?

Appendix 2—Useful Organisations

Alcohol Concern
Waterbridge House
32 Loman Street
London SE1 0EE

**Northern Ireland
Council on Alcohol**
40 Elmswood Avenue
Belfast BT9 6AZ

**Scottish Council on
Alcohol**
137-143 Sauchiehall St.
Glasgow G2 3EW

Alcohol Action Wales
Brunel House 8th Floor
2 Fitzallan House
Cardiff CF2 1EB

Health Education
Authority
Hamilton House
Mabledon Place
London WC1X 9TX

Alcoholics Anonymous
PO Box 1
Stonebow House
York
YO1 2UJ

Al-Anon
61 Great Dover Street
London SE1 4YF

**Women's Alcohol
Centre**
66a Drayton Park
London N5 1ND

**Ethnic Alcohol
Counselling Hounslow**
(EACH)
170a Heston Road
Heston
Middlesex
TW5 0QU

Turning Point
New Loom House
101 Back Church Lane
London E1 1LU

Appendix 3—Useful Books & Training Packs

Camberwell Council on Alcoholism   *Women and Alcohol.* Tavistock, 1980

Goddard, E   *Drinking in England and Wales in the Late 1980's.* HMSO, 1991

Kent, R   *Say When! Everything a Woman Needs to Know About Alcohol.* Sheldon Press, 1989

McConville, B   *Women Under The Influence.* Grafton Books, 1991

Nolan, G & Day, C   *Alcohol & The Black Communities.* DAWN

Alcohol Concern   *Teaching About Alcohol Problems.* Alcohol Concern, 1987

Goodman, C & Ward, M   *Alcohol Problems in Old Age.* Staccato Books, 1989

Homer, A & Gilleard C   *Abuse of Elderly People by their Carers.* British Medical Journal Vol 301 15 Dec 1990 pp1359-1362

Alcohol Concern   *Alcohol Services Directory.* Alcohol Concern, 1993

Edwards, G   *The Treatment of Drinking Problems.* Grant MacIntyre, 1982

Royal College of General Practitioners   *Alcohol & the Public Health.* RCGP, 1991

Royal College of Psychiatrists   *Alcohol Our Favourite Drug.* Tavistock, 1987

Royal College of Physicians   *A Great & Growing Evil.* Tavistock, 1987

Alcohol Training Project   *Alcohol Awareness: Towards A Transcultural Approach* Alcohol Training Project, 1990

Velleman, R   *Counselling For Alcohol Problems.* Sage, 1992

Heather, N & Robertson, I   *Problem Drinking: The New Approach.* Oxford Medical Publications, 1989

Robinson, J   *The Demon Drink.* Methuen, 1988

Appendix 4—References from the main text

1. Robinson, J *The Demon Drink.* Methuen, 1988
2. Drink Pocket Book
3. Institute of Fiscal Studies 1989
4. Unpublished private research by author into annual reports of major UK drinks companies
5. *Older Homeless People in London.* Age Concern. London, 1991
6. Joan Hutten *Short Term Contracts in Social Work.* RKP, 1977
7. Alcohol Concern *Teaching About Alcohol Problems.* Alcohol Concern, 1987
8. J.O. Prochaska & C. C. Di Clementi *Towards a Comprehensive Model of Change*–in *Treating Addictive Behaviours* by W. Miller and N. Heather. Plenum, 1986
9. Homer, A & Gilleard C *Abuse of Elderly People by their Carers.* British Medical Journal Vol 301 15 Dec 1990 pp1359-1362